PLANET🪐KAREN

First Contact

Soaring Penguin Ltd.
London UK

Planet Karen First Contact
by Karen Ellis

Published by
Soaring Penguin Ltd.
4 Florence Terrace
Kingston Vale
London
SW15 3RU
www.soaringpenguin.co.uk

First Edition: October 2009

10 9 8 7 6 5 4 3 2 1

ISBN: 9780955287152

Printed in the UK

Planet Karen Introduction

Take a seat, stranger, and let me tell you why I am an idiot.

It has to do with the book you are now holding in your hands, and how the work in it made me rethink what comics are, and better yet, what they could be.

Flashback a couple years ago. I was a relatively newbie comic book writer, and in my newbie arrogance, I foundnd myself often proselytizing on message boards about potential new markets and formats for comics, new delivery systems to put those books into the hands of potential artists. At the time, I fancied myself a bit of an egalitarian, in that I made no distinction between the great painted European albums, the intensely personal Asian books, the brilliant and swervy independent self-published black and white comics of North America, the bombastic superhero 'mainstream' publishers that I primarily worked for, and the beautifully grubby mini-comics that were often handed to me by guys who look slightly serial-killerish under harsh convention lighting.

It's all comics, I said. That's the beauty of this industry. Find me a human being with eyes, a mind, and a soul, and I'll find you a comic that fits them.

But webcomics?

I'll pass, I thought.

I confess, I just didn't get them. It felt weird to me to read comics on my computer. Can't stick it in my purse, can't read it in the bathtub. No crinkle of pages as you flip forward in the story. Everything seems an odd fit...the horizontal orientation of the average monitor which defies the decades of history that I've invested in reading American comics seems a little sacrilegious somehow.

So, for all my preaching about, "It's all COMICS," I have to say, I went into the whole webcomics readership deal with a big sack of prejudice. And the first few strips that were recommended to me didn't help... there were some adventure strips that seemed merely trying to take the long-gone newspaper daily strip concept and graft it into a format where it fit awkwardly when it fit at all, and the first humor strips that were suggested for me to read did the same with the newspaper gag strips, to an equally mixed (I felt) level of success. Everything felt stuck in two worlds, and somehow incomplete for all the sincerity that may have gone into those early attempts. I felt like my prejudices were never going to be disproved.

It was Karen Ellis who opened my eyes.

Hers was the first webcomic I fell in love with, the first appointment strip I'd come across. I checked out her site and was hooked from the first day, hooked so badly that I immediately went back to the very beginning and read every single panel. And then I went fangirling all over the net telling people about her.

In her very first strip, she summarizes what I think is THE essential question the artist needs to ask her/himself: "I wonder how far I can take it?"

Let me answer that for her—very, very %^&*ing far indeed.

Planet Karen is deceptive and seductive. If you pick a single strip at random, you may get the sense that it's simply an autobiographical gag strip, but it is so much more. Karen takes the tiniest Polaroids of her life, and presents them to everyone with an honesty that is often heartbreaking. She plucks a single moment from the millions we all live through each day and freezes it, holds it up to the light, and reveal the worlds within. She has an addiction for the truth that is at once glorious and a little frightening, and the ferocity and talent to pull it off 's particularly thrilling to see her reach farther and farther as the strip oes on. The drawing evolves mightily, but so too does the writing and he conceptualizing and the boldness of her layouts. The sack of skill ets she has exhibited is brain-spinning, as she shows clearly that she as the courage of the diarist, the deadshot eye of the photographer, he welcome acidity of the satirist, and the unending charm of eliberate self-mocking clown. When she's sad, she tells us so in a way hat is as powerful as it may be indirect, with the vocabulary of the est kind of writer, the ones that never lie to the reader. When she's appy, you can't help but laugh along with her. In Karen's hands, a strip bout eating soup from the pan is as compelling as one about a trip to he hospital. It must be great to see the world through her eyes, as I magine she sees a lot more wonder than the rest of us.

ince Karen showed me it could be done, I've become a fan of several reat webcomics; PVP, Penny Arcade, Narbonic, and many others, ut she was the first to make me see the potential of the format, and or that, I'm very thankful. Like I said, I was an idiot, but at least I've otten a little wiser in this one particular regard.

 can't think of any greater compliment than to say that Karen knows xactly where the words and lines go on the page to make something xtraordinary, and she's got me dying to know where she's going next.

/ery, very %^&*ing far indeed, I bet.

ail Simone is the multiple award-winning, critically acclaimed writer of Wonder Woman, Secret Six, Birds of Prey, Simpsons, and many other comics titles. She has also written for animation, video games, and film. She lives on the Oregon coast with her husband, son, and two stinky dogs.

Andy was talking about the idea of doing a diary as a comic.

He was so enthusiastic about it that I couldn't resist doing one as a parody.

And yet somehow I found something in it beyond the joke.

So this is me going for it. I wonder how far I can take it?

However far it goes, This is my life.

01/03/06

So it was like 3AM and it occured to me I hadn't eaten anything since Lunch.

Silence

I didn't even feel Hungry but I thought I better eat **SOMETHING** so I had some soup.

And I'm tasting it to see if it like needs some salt & pepper which **OF COURSE** it does because tin soup is so bland.

And then I'm like if I'm **SO** not hungry then how come I've just eaten **the whole thing** out of the saucepan before it's even cooked?

Empty

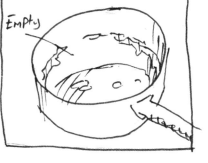

02/03/06

03/03/06

Went to dinner with Chrissie & Rob tonight

we all got totally **WASTED**

After Rob had gone off for a sleep chrissie told me she'd had a misscarriage but Rob didn't know.

Except Rob hadn't gone. He had just passed out behind the Sofa.

GRARRR!!

He was like a mad Zombie on crack!!

I ran and locked Myself in the Loo for an hour.

04/03/06

Band Practice today.
I'm the new girl so it's
Frustrating because it's
Hard to keep up Sometimes

Still Cool though.

Jade is the Lead
Singer. She's a total
attention whore and
She's thin as a stick.

Bitch.

I wonder if she knows
I Fancy her?

05/03/06

07/03/06

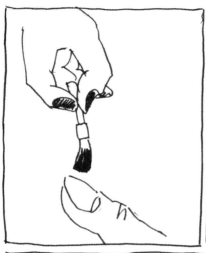

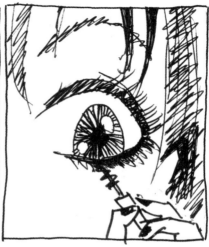

=sigh=

There are days when all the black nail Polish and Mascara in the World won't make it better.

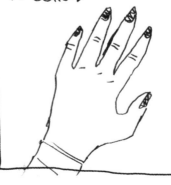

So cold today.

Frozen

It wasn't until I went outside that I saw it had been snowing.

Isn't it supposed to be spring by now? It's so cold that I can't think about anything but how cold it is.

NEW Rule: Snow days are exempt from diets.

09/03/06

10/03/06

Went out clubbing.

Met a guy called Eric or Derek. Alec, maybe. He was cute, anyhow.

Had a **WICKED** time. From what I remember, anyway. I got a li'l wasted.

POUND POUND POUND

BEEP BEEP BEEP

Some of it is kinda vague.

11/03/06

Dragged myself out to Tai Chi. I usually get a ride with Ruth but she wasn't there tonight so I had to walk home.

It's a quiet residential area and it never bothered me before, but suddenly I remembered something Ruth said last week...

I'd rather be in a busy area even if there's drunks about these empty streets are way more creepy.

Thanks so much, Ruth.

13/03/06

Work was so totally dull tonight it was "to die from" as Rika puts it.

I Found some elastic bands So I tried Out some different hairstyles.

So Marge Comes in at 7 a.m. and says

Your hair Looks really stupid Like that.

But she's a hatchet faced old bitch with a fake tan.

I Like it.

And if it Pisses off Marge, that's Just a bonus.

14/03/06

The Comics Workshop.

All the best robots are British

What about Data?

Does HAL count?

Kryten is Welsh

It's easy to reach Geek Overload.

Tonight we were doing a diary day in 4 panels. I didn't do one.

It's more fun down the Pub afterwards.

Anyone know where I can get a cheap monitor?

I could get you one for £100.

IF I had £100 there wouldn't be a problem.

There aren't enough cars named after body parts. I want to drive a Renault spleen

How about a Citroen Duodenum?

A Ford Aesophogus?

Shit. I have to be at work in half an hour.

16/03/06

17/03/06

Today disappeared while I was drawing.

Apart from catching up on my diary, I've been working on some ideas for **"Greetings cards for people you hate."**

Ruth loaned me a monitor. It's smaller than my old one, but has the distinct advantage of actually working.

It's so nice to get caught up on stuff.

19/03/06

My Guilty Secret

When I started doing TaiChi the movements reminded me of dance steps

And I could hear this song playing in my head.

So while it might look like I'm performing a series of tai chi kata,

What I'm **really** doing...

Prince Charming Prince Charming Ridicule is nothing to be scared of

is dancing in an **Adam Ant** video.

20/03/06

21/03/06

I was Just finishing dinner when...

-SNAP

That can't be good.

For some reason my first thought was "Did I brush my teeth this morning?"

I guessed it was the crown had gone, but it was the tooth next to that.

Piece of tooth

filling

Part of it had snapped off.

It didn't hurt. But for a while I could only stare at it.

My tooth! It should be inside my head, not outside!

I think I was a little in shock.

22/03/06

23/03/06

It was warmer today but didn't stop raining all day.

I opened my umbrella but it looked more like Modern art than Something to keep the rain out.

My keyboard refuses to print the letters "i" and "k".

STUP d   eyboard!

All this and the Soles are coming apart on my new Doc Marten's

Can I send this week back? I think it's defective.

24/03/06

According to this thing I read, I am way too needy and so I'm never going to have a successful relationship and I'll die alone.

:sigh:

I was all set to get thoroughly depressed when **Mari** showed up unexpectedly (as always).

darling! **LOVE** the hair!

We went down the pub and did some **serious** research into finding the best mixer for vodka.

Last I recall ginger beer was ahead on points but it gets kinda fuzzy around there.

I think I fell down.

Me too. :Giggle:

25/03/06

It's **Mother's Day** today. My mother is dead.

Thanks **SO MUCH** for the reminder.

I got a new umbrella from **Asda** and went for a walk in the rain down by the river.

There was a life preserver lying on the bank with a rope hanging down from the bridge overhead.

I felt like a background character in someone else's story.

26/03/06

Slept really badly.

Didn't remember the clocks had gone back until I went for my dentist appointment.

Couldn't get another one until **Next Thursday.**

Something about new regulations changing their schedules. It was all **BS.**

I'm going back to bed.

27/03/06

I had this weird dream. I am at this party and everyone is wearing a Superman costume except me.

For some reason I've come dressed as Hawkgirl.

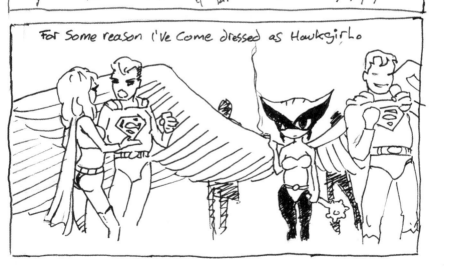

28/03/06

29/03/06

Down the Pub everyone had settled in the non-smoking area so I was stuck on my own...

Hey, Karen.

Come to join me in the smokers' ghetto?

It'll be non-smoking everywhere soon.

We'll all have to huddle outside in the rain

... but not for long.

Whoever heard of scaring them with salami?

Wasn't it that movie?

Oh wait. That was robots.

30/03/06

Went up to London even though it felt like I had a cold coming on

I saw **China Rose!** They totally rocked!

After the gig I ~~was~~

Something bad happened.

I don't want to talk about it right now.

31/03/06

I felt so sick.
I remember wandering through Islington at like 5a.m.

I stopped at the station to wash my face. They have like disposable toothbrushes.

I don't really remember the journey back.

When I got home I put the kettle on, but I fell asleep before it had boiled.

01/04/06

The problem with living alone is that there's no one to look after you when you're ill.

No one to make you chicken soup and no one to tell you you're in no fit state to go shopping for some.

I bought a few odd things that seemed totally reasonable at the time.

It was only when I got home that I realised I'd left my umbrella behind.

Crap.

03/04/06

Felt **SO** much better today it was unreal.

I went back to the supermarket to ask about my umbrella.

It's short and black.

CUSTOMER SERVICE

There's this one.

It wasn't **quite** the one I'd started out with. But it was close enough.

04/04/06

I smoke too much.

Okay I know I have a couple of other vices but I can't afford this one

which is a really crap reason to give up but what can you do?

So I got some of those Nicotine Patch things and stuck one on my arm,

It's supposed to last 24 hours but it fell off 5 minutes later.

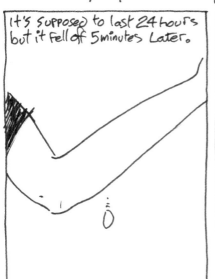

I got it to stay on eventually, though.

05/04/06

I went for my dental appointment and they wanted to charge me **£20** for missing the last one!

I almost walked out but knew I'd never get around to doing anything about it till it started hurting.

But their machine kept refusing my card and after four tries I was later for this one than the one they were charging me for.

Funny how things work out sometimes.

06/04/06

They come to me on the brink of sleep.

Bad things. Fears. Memories of pain.

They call to me

But in my dream I have claws of intricate device.

I slash and tear, and they are gone once more.

07/04/06

The non-smoking thing is going okay. I guess.

The patches work Really well.

But only when I remember to use them.

08/04/06

So I've been reading Stephen King's **Dark Tower** books for what seems like forever.

And as I get to the end of the last volume and the tower comes in sight

What is the thought that enters my head?

ChildeRoland to the dark tower came... and all I got was this stupid T-shirt

09/04/06

I'm having a big Spring clean today. There's some boxes in the closet I haven't opened since I moved in.

I decided to be ruthless and throw out all the crap and take all those books I never read to the charity shop.

So why is it that however much I get rid of, it feels like I still had more than I started with?

:sigh:

10/04/06

I had this weird conversation with Mari today.

It was like we talked for hours but never actually said anything.

Is something up with her or is it me?

11/04/06

First issue came back from the printers today!

PLANET KAREN

I was so **excited** to see what it looked like.

Unfortunately Andy had got the interiors printed A6 as planned but the covers were **A5**.

You're going to put this in the comic, aren't you?

They'll make good promotional flyers though.

Oh, **totally**.

12/04/06

I was just falling asleep when I had this idea for a comic.

I remember going through it in my head, panel by panel.

But when I woke up I had totally lost it.

shit

So I resolved from now on to keep a pad and pen by the bed just in case.

13/04/06

So there I was, chilling to **Yoshimi Battles the Pink Robots** when this thought pops out of nowhere.

I should apply to art college

I mean, It's not the first time this has crossed my mind, but before it had always been theoretical

I looked up the University of W.O.E. on the net and requested an application.

It's a little scary.

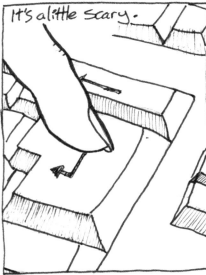

I so need new shoes. My sneakers have suddenly got so tight it's painful and I can't afford new ones.

All my money seems to be going on pens, paper, sketchbooks, pencils, brushes, erasers, inks....

How to tell you are a real artist:

① You spend more on art materials than ~~shoes~~ food.

18/04/06

Okay, I admit it.

There are times when stubborn optimism will only get you so far.

Bip Beep Bip Bip Beep

Hello? Yes, I'd like to make an appointment for the giving up smoking clinic.

19/04/06

Today was one of those busy days. Dentist first. All went smoothly for a change. I kept my eyes shut

GRRRNND BZZZ whiiirr

I Like my dentist but I don't want to watch her work,

Paused only to try and eat soup with half my face numb, then off to the doctor. Stopped at the supermarket on the way home even though I could barely see from the drops the doctor had put in my eyes.

Probably wasn't the best day to have offered to cook dinner.

But I finally got to relax at the movies.

20/04/06

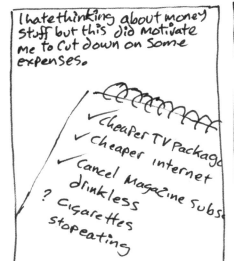

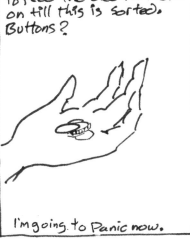

21/04/06

Andy called and made the mistake of asking how I was.

How long have you got?

I may not be great at asking for help but I'm not too stubborn to accept when it's offered.

That would be cool.

He loaned me a tenner, which will at least keep the electric running for a while.

FEEEED MEEE!!

And I was able to help him out assembling some of the comics he was publishing (including mine), so that was cool.

22/04/06

One of the comics I was assembling was Sally's diary comic, which was what prompted me to start this in the first place.

It's interesting to see how differently we approach the same idea.

I eventually finished all the collating, folding, & stapling.

So I spent the rest of the day playing video games.

23/04/06

Checked my account online this morning.

Some money had gone in. Yay!!

YOU'RE NOT BROKE!

After covering the overdraft and the charges there wasn't much left.

=sigh=

But at least I won't starve.

Beans for tea again I guess.

24/04/06

"Smoking Sessation" clinic.

When d you want to be your start date?

How about today?

I expected the therapist to be sympathetic and supportive but she made me feel like I was eight years old.

Well it can't be today because you already had one.

Um, tomorrow, then?

She even gave me homework.

CiGiES are eViL!

But she also gave me a prescription for more patches, which was what I really wanted.

25/04/06

26/04/06

Andy tried to get me down the pub.

Not tonight.

But I don't like going out with no money in my pocket.

Poor thing

And then there's the whole cigarette thing.

HSSS!

So I'll just have a quiet night in.

28/04/06

So here we are at the end of another month.

I have 3 pages in various stages of completion and I haven't finished the cover.

And there's a bunch of stuff still waiting to get scanned

I really like doing this, but the schedule is very unforgiving.

29/04/06

I slept for like 3 hours, then it was back to the drawing board.

Two hours later I had to get out for a walk to clear my head.

I took a wrong turn and found myself in a little graveyard I'd never seen before.

WOW!

I *totally* have to come back here with my sketchbook.

30/04/06

I found the University online application today.

The bad news is that I can't fill in a lot of the details as I no longer have that information.

Examining board? I'm not even sure what school it was.

The other bad news is that I don't have anyone qualified to be a reference.

The **OTHER** bad news is that the main deadline was two months ago.

I think I might just blow this week's housekeeping on a bottle of Vodka.

Thud

02/05/06

I was off out sketching today when I got distracted.

oooh

OUTLAW
open Casting Call

It was just around the corner in a gloomy cafe. I had to fill in a form.

Within a few minutes a guy was telling me how he could get me in a movie with Sean Bean and Bob Hoskins.

They took a photo and that was it.

I auditioned for a part in a **movie!** **wheee!!**

R237

03/05/06

04/05/06

Free Comic Book Day! I got a stack of all kinds of stuff I don't usually read.

There was this one comic where all the women were drawn like 16 year old anorexics with implants.

I am **SO** tempted to do a parody.

You could call it **Surgically Enhanced Anorexic Bimbos.**

Too eighties.

Their kryptonite would be **Twinkies** and their arch-enemy would be **Ronald McDonald!**

06/05/06

I suddenly got in a panic about my lettering.

My lettering sucks.

I tried typesetting a couple of pages to see how it looked.

Fish for tea?

Issue #2 goes to the printers tomorrow. Do I have time to re-letter all thirty pages?

I'd almost made up my mind when I sent them to David.

Your lettering is fine as it is.

It's always interesting when someone you rely on to give a straight answer gives you a straight answer.

Oh.

I'll stop panicking then.

07/05/06

The dentist was 20 minutes late seeing me today. Does that mean they owe me £20 now?

Sometimes I wonder what's going on just below my line of sight.

But only sometimes.

She said I shouldn't eat on that side for a day or two.

But I have a temporary filling on the other side too.

So I guess that'll be soup for dinner this week.

08/05/06

My big Sister Sent me Some money, bless her.

I bought Shoes and Vodka.

I had a nap and dreamed about Shoes and Sex.

The Shoes were better.

Draw Your own Conclusion.

Huh?

09/05/06

My MP3 Player plays audio-book files in random order.

Unless I rename the file names to numbers.

It's quite a surreal narrative experience

Have you considered a career in piracy?

You're trying to kidnap what I've rightfully stolen.

There's not a lot of money in revenge.

Huh?

Especially when I am all fluffy-headed from caffienne defficiency

I knew there was something I forgot to get yesterday.

:shake:
:shake:

So... wait, what was I talking about, again?

neeed brains... er, coffeee...

10/05/06

Celebrated David's birthday at **Zero Degrees** microbrewery.

Happy birthday David!

They do this amazing **Mango** beer.

cheers!

There was a noisy crowd next to us who seemed to be giving each other medals.

Turned out they had just won the national **Frisbee** championship.

11/05/06

The Con was kinda bigger than I expected.

It was **SO cool** to see people buying my stuff.

I had a **Crossover** moment with **Sally**.

I'm not sure if I read your comic it might influence how I do mine.

It felt like at least one of us was fictional.

I felt the same when I read yours.

13/05/06

Someone at the Con was telling me how fans are making themed sketchbooks now.

They get guest artists to all draw the same thing or include some specific element.

There's this one guy who just wants a **cliff** in the picture.

I couldn't resist it.

I got **Stick Figures!**

14/05/06

I'M not **exactly** a morning person. To me, **sunrise** is nature's way of telling you it's time to go to **bed**.

KO-FEE

It was a busy weekend, and I didn't get much time to draw, and I have a whole **new** bunch of ideas I want to work on.

KO-FEE GUD

So I **really** need to get working on that while it's all **fresh** and **exciting**.

Just as soon as the higher brain functions kick in.

MORE KO-FEE

15/05/06

Usually, coming up with ideas is hard work.

Princess Pallindrome's costume should have a symetrical type theme

Today I can barely keep up with them

Anagram girl has to say spells in anagrams. Like Zatanna only not.

I keep having to stop what I'm doing to note things down.

Muses For Hire or The Muse Agency?

Days like this are rare and precious

My throat is so sore. I SO don't have time to be ill.

:Cough:

16/05/06

My nose is blocked and my mouth feels like something died in it.

My throat was so sore, all I could stand to eat all day was chocolate chip Weetabix.

I slept a lot, too. I even dreamed how this comic finished, but it was gone the moment I opened my eyes.

All I could remember was that in the last panel I was dressed as **Batgirl**.

I have no clue why.

17/05/06

I went out to get ice cream to soothe my poor sore throat.

Yum

There were some guys outside the **HIPPODROME** protesting Jerry Springer the Opera.

So have you even seen the show?

I've read leaflets.

HIPPODROME

THE BLOOD OF JESUS CHRIST

18/05/06

19/05/06

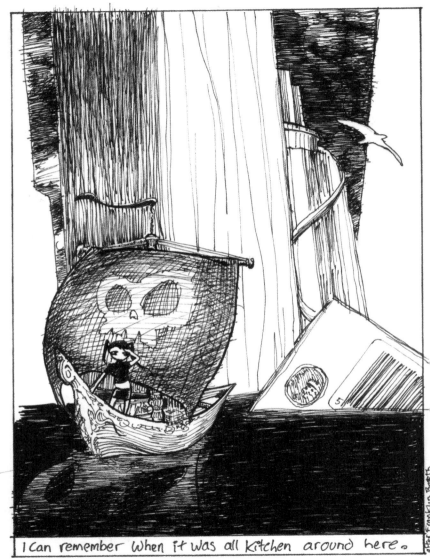

I can remember when it was all kitchen around here.

20/05/06

There seem to be a lot of Flags about today.

inflatable armchairs?

I guess there must be some sporty thing happening.

You can tell it's not just people being patriotic.

In England when you want to be patriotic you wave around the Union Jack.

You only get expressive with the Flag of St.George for Sports events.

21/05/06

22/05/06

It's been a month since I ran out of money, so I checked my bank account online.

The good news is that I'm winning.

Yay me.

Not by much, but I've pulled it back from the brink.

So I'll be living on rice and soup for a while longer. I can't afford to buy anything unless I sell something else first, and my social life remains in the toilet.

So how do I feel?

I'm on top of the world.

Trying not to slip off.

23/05/06

24/05/06

25/05/06

26/05/06

I **want** to go to Diane's **Party** tonight, but I know she invited Tris

She **knows** if he goes I won't go but she **always** asks me anyway

Does her putting the decision on **me** save her from choosing between her friends?

If she invites me when I've said **no way** will I go then she's not responsible when I do **exactly** what I've said I'll do all along.

So I get to **angst** all day about a decision I **already** made and end up not going anyway.

Blah.

27/05/06

Ruth got a Chocolate Fountain for a hen party she's going to

So you dip stuff in the melted chocolate?

I've got a big jar of cherries in brandy, some pineapple chunks, marshmallows, and some little biscuit things. And four pounds of chocolate.

How about little sticks of carrot and celery?

Huh?

You know, for people who want a healthy option.

29/05/06

30/05/06

I am out late at night

I wear my big (leather biker) jacket

I walk with my fists balled ready to step into a **Jeet Kune Do** defensive stance.

I am not a target.

31/05/06

01/06/06

I was very dull today. I spent most of it finishing up issue #3 for publication, reformatting the pictures and adding the title page and all that fun stuff.

I've got a new host for the online version. It's going to take a lot of work to fix up the site.

I was surfing the web when my attention wandered, and I found this gallery of some guy who commissions artists to do illustrations of his fanfic character.

And suddenly it occured to me:

I'm an artist. I could do that!

03/06/06

Sometimes
I feel so
isolated.

I can't remember
the last time I
touched someone

04/05/06

How could anyone possibly be addicted to Flapjacks?

Sainsbury's had these on two for one when I was ill, so I got some as comfort food.

mmm. Flapjacks

TWO FOR Flapjacks + cupcakes

I've been stuffing them by the box ever since and now the offer is finished.

I'm getting worse cravings than I did for the cigarettes.

EEAT MEEE!

MUST RESIST!

SMALL CAKE

05/06/06

I got my first Commission!

A Pirate Bear?!?

I'd only written about it on the website yesterday and had totally no idea what to expect.

Neither bears nor pirates are exactly my speciality, but I live five minutes walk from the main Public Library

Now this is my idea of a fulfilling job. Getting paid to do something you really enjoy.

06/06/06

My sleep/wake cycle has got completely out of control.

it's What time?

YAWN

Decided the only way to fix it was to stay up long enough to go to bed at the right time.

More Coffee

Funny how time drags when you haven't the brain to do anything interesting.

I think I read this Page before.

Several times.

Ah, Video games. what better mindless waste of time was ever created?

07/06/06

In World War two a lot of **bombs** got dropped on Bristol.

The traffic's backed up for miles.

They just **found** one of them.

Yes, there's Police and firemen everywhere. they've got the whole area Cordoned off

It's frantic.

So there's no way I can get in.

Okay, I will

bye.

It's not often you get such a **brilliant** excuse on such a sunny day. It would be a crime not to use it.

08/06/06

09/06/06

I can't help but notice that the world cup has started

The inhabitants of nearby pubs are keen to share the game progress with the rest of the world.

ONE NILL!
ONE NILL!
CON
ENG

The only reason I care about the score is so that I'll know whether the drunk fans roaming the city will be in a good mood or a bad one when I go out.

ODEON

I never did find out who won.

Good thing we stayed to the end.

10/06/06

I went to an art show today.

It seemed to involve images and video of a young black guy pretending to be an old black woman.

Apparently it was intended "to evoke the tragedy of the typecast actor doomed to recreate and replay the same role", specifically Hattie McDaniel who played Mamie in Gone With the Wind.

Which was an interesting idea but all I could see on display was the role, not the tragedy.

11/06/06

12/06/06

So I was at this comic shop where they sell my comic and this guy comes up to me and asks

Is it true?

What do you mean? Like do four little pictures give an accurate factual record of every twenty four hour period of my life?

Or am I just **Making** it **UP** and none of it really happened?

And **What** difference would it make **to your Life** either way?

13/06/06

Surprised myself today. Planet Karen has been taking up so much time lately I haven't had the energy for much else.

Then today I had an idea for a story and just sat down and sketched out the whole thing.

Wow! I've just drawn eight pages.

Later I met some friends down the pub.

But he's not so good good with anatomy.

Which is harsh coming from his girlfriend

HAHA HAHA

Did I miss something?

Nothing important, dear.

14/06/06

Got a letter from the bank telling me they bounced my rent cheque

What the F[

I checked online and it seems they charged me £60 for when I went over my limit. Right now I'm living on less than half that per week.

I wanted to keep the little money I've made from commissions and stuff to buy art materials and for when the computer breaks down.

SELF DESTRUCT
10
SECONDS

Now I'm going to have to use that money to pay the rent.

Crap.

16/06/06

I hate having arguments but I'm very opinionated

It's not a good combination

I submitted a proposal to a Feminist Small Press Project because I thought I could contribute something useful.

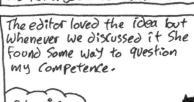

The editor loved the idea but whenever we discussed it she found some way to question my competence.

Patronising cow.

I withdrew my proposal, but I made my feelings clear.

HAHAHAHAHAHAHAHA...

Kirbytech™
For when
overkill
is the only
solution

17/06/06

A wonderful friend in Texas got me a free trial of **World of Warcraft**.

"Cool."

It took five hours to **download**.

Forty five minutes to **unpack**.

An hour to **install**.

And **then** it started **Patching**.

♪ When there's trouble you know who to call ♪

And then it wouldn't add the final patch because there was no room left on the hard drive

"Huh? I had **eight gigs** free this morning."

"Give me back my **gigabytes** you stupid machine!"

18/06/06

My adventures in **WoW** Continue Today I am **Necromonica**, an **Undead** (kinda like a Zombie).

I Continue to Find the Unlikeliest objects inside Creatures I defeat

And For Someone **already** dead I seem to die a lot.

GRR

But it's Fun Stealing Pumpkins and Picking Flowers

I need a bigger Sack.

Nearly gave up on **WOW** today. I got killed and spent hours roaming the world as a ghost.

WOOOOOOOOooooooooo I am **SO** Lost.

Whenever I got near my body there seemed to be impassable hills in the way.

Wait. Is it a left here or what?

Later I went on a ride in a Zepplin and explored an Underground city

sit!

I am a Fantasy tourist.

21/06/06

I've been so wrapped up in myself lately I completely failed to notice yesterday was summer solstice

I feel like I should have danced naked around a tree or gone on a picnic.

Or at least looked at a calendar.

22/06/06

It's kinda weird how things develop sometimes.

Planet Karen started out as a monthly print comic.

I just did the web version as an afterthought.

Four months later the webcomic has more daily readers than there are copies of the print edition

I could stop doing a print version altogether and hardly notice.

My comic! Mine!

But there's something about comics you can hold.

23/06/06

24/06/06

25/06/06

26/06/06

"*People wonder where the joy in comics has gone. I'll tell you where--Karen's got it. She took it when we weren't looking and has ingeniously injected it into even her darkest strips. Great stuff that gives me hope for the future.*"

Gail Simone

I feel like flying.

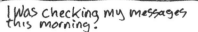

I was checking my messages this morning:

- ☐ spam
- ☐ spam
- ☐ Gail Simone
- ☐ offer to host Planet Karen at girl-wonder.org
- ☐ invitation to closed beta of new online game.

I think I broke my brain.

In the evening I met some friends down the pub.

29/06/06

A year ago I was adrift with no direction and no hope.

Four months ago.

IF I can just keep this up for a month, I'll have enough to make a mini-comic.

Today I feel like I have a future.

30/06/06

It's **SO** hot.
In Summer my studio is a total heat trap.

Even at 3am it's still so hot that I'm sweating just sitting at the drawing board.

I have to be careful not to drip on the picture I'm drawing.

AirConditioning would be nice. But it's not all bad.

Ice Cream
4 teh Win

01/07/06

A lot of what I read on the net lately is like Cosmo for Comics.

I spend way too much time looking at it when I should be doing other things.

The sooner it comes in a portable, waterproof format, the better.

02/07/06

In times of stress I often think to myself **W.W.W.W.D.?**

But since this usually suggests bondage, execution, or twirling

around until I get dizzy, it's rarely of any practical use.

03/07/06

04/07/06

It's still hot. But it's England in the Summertime so rain was inevitable

Maybe i'll just get my umbrella.

For once it's not raining in the kitchen.

No. Today it's in the studio.

Could be worse. At least it's been clear of the computer and the drawing board. So far.

05/07/06

I dream I have mislaid Barbara Gordon's Phone number.

I wake up to find the Power is out.

The rain has reached the electric Sockets in the Kitchen.

This is not a good Way to start the day.

06/07/06

It's Jess and Darko's Farewell Party.

I haven't known them long, but we really made a connection.

Isn't that the guitarist from Sisters of Mercy?

It was an excellent party

We danced all night

Hi.

Hi.

07/07/06

PLANET KAREN

I'm Karen and this is my diary.
PlanetKarenComic
@googlemail.com

Day Date Month

Comic goes here

HOME
COMMISSIONS
F.A.Q.
ARCHIVES
LINKS

FORUM

[Make a Donation]

Current donation gift

If you like this comic and think more people should see it, or if you just want to see the *cool extra* junk, hit these buttons:

TOP WEB COMICS
Vote 167

BUZZCOMIX TOP 100
VOTE

Text here for news or footnote to curr strip and blah de blah waffle like tha a bit.

XML feed

All w   es
Com

Commission link GALLERY

09/07/06

It's not easy to come up with something insightful or witty every single day.

Plus (as I've mentioned before) I tend to forget stuff if I don't write it down quick.

Oh MY God! that's like the most profound thing ever!

So I keep a notebook with me all the time

Here's my trusty notebook, and...

Sometimes I even remember to take a working pen.

Crap.

10/07/06

I got home at 2am. Yay me, I have a social life

At 8am. they started digging up the street outside.

CRASH
WHUMP
DRIIIIII

RUMBLE
DRIIIIIILL
CRASH
WHIIIIIIIE
BANG

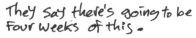

They say there's going to be four weeks of this.

GRIIIIND
KRR
THUMP
BUZZ!

11/07/06

It's Emma's driving test today. We arranged to go out for a drink afterwards to celebrate or commiserate.

She said she'd call me to let me know where to meet.

She hadn't called by 9:30 so I tried phoning her.

Hello, Emma's machine. When you see Emma can you tell her Karen called?

Thanks. Bye.

At least I got lots of work done while I was waiting.

12/07/06

Got an email from Emma this morning.

She apologised for yesterday and then
broke our date for tonight to go see
Pirates of the Caribbean

Screw it

I'm going anyway.

13/07/06

Today I passed a truck that had crashed, scattering its cargo of flowers.

Further on I found a chess set all set up by the side of the road. Several of the pieces have had their heads chopped off.

If this is all a metaphor, I wish someone would explain it to me.

14/07/06

The noise outside mostly died down once they finished digging up the street.

But now and again I am treated to a Symphony for buzz-saw or whatever.

Oddly, I've never actually seen them working there.

It's like they all run away and hide when I go outside.

18/07/06

David loaned me this audio tape of **Lord of the Ages** by Magna Carta.

My only working cassette player is in the kitchen, so I didn't get around to listening to it until now

> The Lord of the Ages rode one night out through the gateways of time. Astride a great charger, in a cloak of white sammite he flew on the air like a storm.

It's like Spinal Tap's 'Stonehenge' only done totally serious — it's incredible this was ever chart material

> Lord of the Ages
> Nobody knows
> Wither he goes
> Nobody knows
> ...her he goes
> ...ther he goes
> ...w he goes

1973 is another planet.

> But the old and the helpless, the weak and the hum...
> to the children of light his words of compassion
> ...them gently, dissolving the darkness
> ...rumbled with fire.
> ...nction, the Lord
> of th... ...of the harvest

HAHAHA

19/07/06

20/07/06

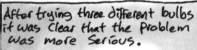

21/07/06

22/07/06

24/07/06

I went down to the library to scan today's comic.

Last thing I had done before my system had gone down was to ask for help on the web.

I logged in to find that there has been close to £300 donated!

I spent the rest of the morning ~~Window shopping~~ pricing up new computers.

LOW!!

SPECIAL OFFER

BUY!!

25/07/06

26/07/06

27/07/06

They started work on the electrics at 8:30. Why do they always do these things so early?

This coffee seems to be cold.

I went for a walk and found a little french street market.

I had deep fried calimari (squid rings) for lunch

When I got home there was a package waiting - it was almost as big as me!

New toys!

It's going to be fun getting this upstairs.

28/07/06

My beautiful new computer! It's a total **beast** of a system. It's like twice the size of my old machine.

There were several alternatives around the same price & spec, but **this** one had **six** fans – three of my big computer problems recently have been down to overheating and this one is so cool I could use it for A.C.

Now I just have to install the operating system, drivers for all the hardware, and all of the programs I use on a daily basis.

Fan Controls

There's no floppy drive, but there is a DVD ROM **and** a DVD writer, two 80gb hard drives 1gb of RAM, and a 3ghz processor.

Plus there was enough money left over to replace my ancient graphics tablet.

29/07/06

30/07/06

Leaving is always hard.

But it's time to move on.

31/07/06

There was this guy. It was kind of a friend of a friend thing.

We talked for hours. We had so much in common.

At the end of the evening he asked if I'd like to go for a drink sometime.

I said no.

Yeah, I was surprised, too.

02/08/06

I live in the heart of the city. It's handy for the shops, but it has its own problems.

Some days I can't get six yards without tripping over a charity fundraiser.

It's hard to believe in their dedication when you see the same guy shilling for different causes every day.

It brings out the snark in me.

I'm not so much a Friend of the Earth - more of an acquaintance.

04/08/06

One thing I don't understand.

If I love drawing my comic (and I do)...

I really must...

I really must get on with the comic.

Why does it take so long to get around to doing it some days?

Soon as I finish this...

05/08/06

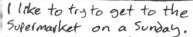

I like to try to get to the supermarket on a Sunday.

There's always a ton of stuff on special offer I couldn't usually afford.

I never know what I'm going to end up having for dinner

Stir fry tonight! And a New York deli wrap for lunch tomorrow.

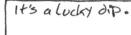

It's a lucky dip.

Fresh cream cakes. I really shouldn't.

.06/08/06

The Construction Crew gave me my usual alarm call.

I open the front door to find they've taken the Street away.

Whoa!

I take this as an omen and decide to Stay home.

Luckily I'd just installed World of Warcraft on the new Computer.

Once upon a time, a poor Princess found a Street of Faded Wonders.

Each shop sold more and stranger junk than the last.

Finally, hidden away at the back of the last and strangest shop

The Princess found some magic slippers that fitted her perfectly.

08/08/06

So I decided to practice with the rollerblades in a more controlled environment.

Somewhere smaller, where no one would see me.

Like my kitchen.

I need to work on those landings.

10/08/06

11/08/06

If it's a choice between minimal art and no comic at all for a few days then I hope you will forgive me if I go for the minimal art thing.

In fact I'd like to take the opportunity to show you a variety of minimal art styles used by professional comic artists.

I thought it might be fun to demonstrate some of the techniques used by comic creators to minimize the artwork load, and I've invited Mari to join me as my beautiful assistant to help me show you how it's done.

Hi there.

Now I want to point out that all the things I'm going to show you are legitimate comic elements,

Well, you would.

There are times when they are the best artistic way of telling the story. It's only when they are overused that they become "cheats".

There are all sorts of techniques that can be artistic shortcuts.

What, like filling the panels with a ton of dialogue so that there is barely any room left for the pictures?

That's right, Mari!

12/08/06

13/08/06

15/08/06

Today we are being invisible. It's always been a problem to depict invisibility in such an essentially visual medium.
Sometimes invisible things are shown as transparent, or with dotted lines. Isn't that right, Mari?
Mari?
Where's that girl got to now? I better go find her.
giggle

16/08/06

17/08/06

And now it's time for the latest installment of the running joke that is my bank account.

This month the bank has charged me £35 for bouncing my rent cheque last month because there wasn't quite enough money in the account to cover it after they had taken out the charges they had stuck me with the previous month.

I'm totally starting to lose the plot here. Can they spin this out another month?

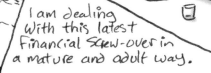

I am dealing with this latest financial screw-over in a mature and adult way.

Vodka, Pizza and a marathon of Godzilla movies.

19/08/06

I've been kinda depressed lately.

I mean depressed to the point where I want to tell everyone to just go away and leave me alone.

Sadly, I haven't seen anyone to tell them this.

20/08/06

I've been playing a lot of **World of Warcraft** lately, and I really enjoy it, but inevitably there are a couple of things about the game that are kinda irritating.

What task would you have me do?

I want you to take the portal to Rut'abega Village, and from there catch the ferry over to Aubergene

When you get there hang a left and run north for twenty minutes until you find my cousin Elbert. He will give you a trivial task to perform to lull you into a false sense of security and then send you south to talk to someone else.

After a forty minute run south you'll be given a quest you can't complete for another five levels.

But on the plus side you'll find the Hippogryph bus stop so you'll be able to fly there next time

What kind of public transport system makes you visit each stop before you can use it?

31/08/06

To be fair, the biggest problem with WOW is that it's just so much fun that it's easy to spend way too much time playing it...

22/08/06

The **Planet Karen** mini-comic seems to have died.

As I reach the end of the pages that would form issue #6, all I have to show for issue #4 is a bunch of covers that were printed up in July.

Of course I'm disappointed.

But it was a lot of extra work for something hardly anyone saw. And for which I've never been paid.

23/08/06

24/08/06

Today it rained.
And rained and rained and rained and rained.
And it all stayed outside.
Yay.

25/08/06

I was all set for an evening of W.O.W. when I remembered about the dance show.

It was tough to drag myself out, but I was glad I did. It was totally **amazing**!

There seemed to be some narrative to the dance but I couldn't tell you what, beyond the romance element.

It was **SO** spectacular! Now I **totally** have to see some **Bollywood** musicals.

If I only had a clue where to start.

26/08/06

I was sorting out a
few bits and pieces
when suddenly it
occured to me that
I had no idea which
things were bits and
which were pieces.

I haven't drawn anything for days and now I'm scared to try.

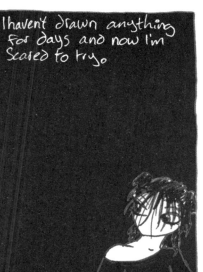

I'm afraid the art has gone away and part of me would rather not try than have it confirmed.

I push myself to sit at the drawing board.

The magic happens again.

31/08/06

01/09/06

's hard to stay totally anonymous or long, even in the middle of a city.

Which is cool, I guess.

Hello Karen. I haven't seen your face around here in a while.

Hi.

Have you been ll? You look pale, even for you.

oh yes, I so want to share my issues with the whole street.

There are just times when I'd rather be invisible.

I'm fine, now.

Just give me my frigging cake.

02/09/06

I'm on the **Telephone Preference** register, so I don't get many junk phone calls.

RING RING

And even when I do, I'm usually Polite. I know the guy on the other end is just doing his job.

No, I don't want a mobile Phone, and you aren't allowed to call and sell me stuff.

This is the third time today I've been called about this, and I haven't got any more interested since last time.

But there are times...

NO! I DO NOT want your FUCKING Phone and WHY are you EVEN still TALKING to me?

03/09/06

It's not so much that I lose track of time as I get too narrowly focussed on other things.

I notice there's a show I like on in half an hour.

Must remember to catch that.

Next time I think of it I hit the remote to see if it's started yet.

Only to realise that two days have passed.

05/09/06

The **Bollywood** DVD I got off **ebay** arrived today.

It turned out to be a homemade copy. And not even in a case.

Okay, it was suspiciously **cheap**, but I'm tempted to report it to ebay.

I'll just **watch** it first to see if the movie is any good.

06/09/06

01809/06

Stuck my head out of my cave long enough to hear that **Lea Hernandez's** house has burned down.

They're organising an art auction to raise funds for her so I'm going to dig out some nice pictures to send them.

I'd email her but I get the impression that everyone and their therapist is doing that right now.

There's something I can do that is actually helpful. I'll do that.

09/09/06

Things are starting to get back to normal and I'm catching up on all the email I got over the last few weeks.

It's weird to be making comics about the dark times - I've never written about it before.

or even thought about it much once it was over.

11/09/06

I spent all night throwing up

It would be some consolation if I'd been doing something truely hedonistic beforehand, but no.

The mere sight (and smell) of the bathroom makes me ill.

I'll clean it up later.

12/09/06

After twenty four hours the fever went down and I started feeling human again.

AAAah!

But I can't see me ever ever eating tomato and three bean soup any more.

I mean, I wouldn't say it was my all time favourite but I ate it quite often.

But food just isn't the same once you've experienced it in reverse.

GRUMBLE

13/09/06

Grey breeze whispers rain
Leaves dance in a sunset sky
Autumn in the air

15/09/06

I've been getting an extreme reaction to chopping onions lately.

It's not only painful but very inconvenient when you have to stop cooking for twenty minutes to go have a good blub.

So I tried this thing I heard about biting down on a wooden spoon.

Kind of hard to believe, but it actually works!

20/09/06

22/09/06

I really wanted **PlanetKaren.com** but it was owned by one of those companies that buy up domain names by the zillion and then sell them on.

I asked how much they wanted for it and they said $1.0880.

oh yes, that is **SO** going to happen.

So I got Planetkaren.co.uk instead.

It cost me $8.

YES!

23/09/06

26/09/06

ppendix

hen I started Planet Karen, the rules I developed for myself were
nple: 1) I had to produce one page of comic to cover events from
e day, to be completed in one day. When the day was over I had to
ove on. 2) it had to be true.

s a great way to avoid getting too precious about your work; too
gged down in perfectionism.

course it also had to be coherent and entertaining, so by "Truth"
ften mean an iconic representation of something that actually
ppened, distilled down to a four panel comic. Or at least how I
efer to recall it happening.

rprisingly, although I managed to produce a comic virtually every
y for the first six months, I also found time to do other things. While
t part of the actual diary, here are a couple of Planet Karen related
ces I did during that time.

st is a spoof advertisement I did as a result of seeing too many
gging TV adverts while ill with a high temperature.

en there's a non-diary Planet Karen strip I did for the small press
mic Scar Tissue 2, and the cover from the same comic.

ren Ellis
gust 2009
stol

PLANET KAREN

by Karen Ellis

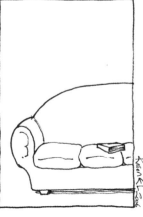